Rainer Maria Rilke
Sonnets to Orpheus

Rainer Maria Rilke
Sonnets to Orpheus

A New English Version,
With a Philosophical Introduction
by
Rick Anthony Furtak

University of Scranton Press
Scranton and London

Library of Congress Cataloging-in-Publication Data

Rilke, Rainer Maria, 1875-1926.
   [Sonette an Orpheus. English]
   Sonnets to Orpheus : a new English version / Rainer Maria Rilke ; with a
philosophical introduction by Rick Anthony Furtak.
      p. cm.
   Includes bibliographical references and index.
· ISBN 978-1-58966-160-8 (cloth : alk. paper)
   1. Orpheus (Greek mythology)--Poetry. I. Furtak, Rick Anthony. II. Title.
   PT2635.I65S613 2008
   831'.912--dc22

                                                                    2007044715

Distribution:
University of Scranton Press
Chicago Distribution Center
11030 S. Langley
Chicago, IL 60628

PRINTED IN THE UNITED STATES OF AMERICA

TABLE OF CONTENTS

DEDICATION AND ACKNOWLEDGMENTS

Rilke characterized these poems as a memorial to Vera Ouckama Knoop, and (while honoring his wishes) I would also like to dedicate this translation to my grandmother Doris Leona Kugler, in honor of her ninetieth birthday.

For their editorial support and encouragement, I am grateful to Simon Lewis of *Illuminations* and to Brent Dean Robbins of *Janus Head*. Most of all, I am indebted to Jeff Gainey, Director of the University of Scranton Press, for the confidence he has shown from the very start.

This project has come together in an unusually solitary space, partly due to my own superstitions about talking too much about it before it was finished. Among the few people who have read part of the manuscript, Karin Nisenbaum deserves both thanks and an apology for my failure to include her name on the acknowledgments page of my first book. Eliana Schoenberg made some valuable suggestions after reading a late draft of the introduction, and Ed Mooney did the same with respect to phrases within a few specific poems. Kiley Dunlap brought up a number of relevant issues during conversations dealing with her undergraduate thesis on Heidegger, as did James Reid during countless exchanges from which I have learned more than I can say. Along the way, I also benefited from discussions with Sarah Pessin and J. P. Rosensweig, and from more indirectly related conversations with Jonathan Ellsworth and Andrew Henscheid. My sister Erin Marie Furtak and my brother-in-law Dave Suss were helpful and patient in advising me about the German language.

I should also thank Carole Oles, Christopher Ricks, Jay Rubin, and Alene Terzian for much poetry-related dialogue and for keeping me connected with the larger world of letters. My summer 2004 class at Deep Springs College not only rekindled my interest in Rilke but also reminded me of why this kind of writing matters. If not for the inspiring environment of that place in the high desert, I might have convinced myself that I no longer had the right kind of divine madness to be composing poetry. My fall 2005 course on philosophy and literature at Colorado College was also a source of stimulating conversations, and Sara Ellsworth allowed me to share impressions about Rilke with a trusted literary companion. I have also learned from many previous translators of Rilke's sonnets, including those whom I critique in these pages. Finally, generous funding from the John D. and Catherine T. MacArthur Foundation played a key role in enabling me to bring this project to completion.

TRANSLATOR'S INTRODUCTION
Rilke and the Poetics of Revelation

Commonly acknowledged as one of the greatest modern poets, Rainer Maria Rilke (1875–1926) also holds a unique place in the philosophical canon. His writings have captured the attention of such major Continental thinkers as Martin Heidegger, Maurice Merleau-Ponty, Hans-Georg Gadamer, and Paul Ricoeur. Passages from Rilke's poetry are used as epigraphs on the front pages of Gadamer's *Wahrheit und Methode* and Ricoeur's *Le Voluntaire et l'involuntaire,*[1] and selections from Rilke's own works appear in two prominent anthologies of existential philosophy. Although Rilke is the only author in either anthology who is remembered primarily as a poet, neither Walter Kaufmann nor Robert Solomon chooses to include any of Rilke's poetry in their collections.[2] Consequently, readers of existential philosophy have often been introduced to Rilke through brief excerpts from *The Notebooks of Malte Laurids Brigge*, a curious book-length

1   Originally published in mid-century, these two texts appear in English as *Truth and Method* and *Freedom and Nature: The Voluntary and the Involuntary*. For the Rilke epigraphs, see Hans-Georg Gadamer, *Truth and Method*, trans. by Joel Weinsheimer and Donald Marshall (London: Continuum, 2004), v; and Paul Ricoeur, *Freedom and Nature*, trans. by Erazim Kohák (Evanston, IL: Northwestern University Press, 1966), ix.

2   See *Existentialism from Dostoevsky to Sartre*, ed. by Walter Kaufmann (New York: Penguin, 1975), 134–41 and *Existentialism*, ed. by Robert Solomon (Oxford: Oxford University Press, 2005), 153–55.

narrative that must be counted as a minor work alongside either of Rilke's poetic masterpieces, *Duino Elegies* and *Sonnets to Orpheus*.

Because one of my goals in this book is to bring Rilke's poetry to a philosophical audience, I should begin by saying a few things about why his writings have already been recognized as part of the existential tradition. In the aforementioned *Notebooks*, Rilke's narrator portrays human life as a state of anguish, confusion, and despair. As he meditates fearfully on the prospect of death, he questions the meaning of things and struggles in vain to "rub off the make-up" and "be real," to develop an authentic sense of identity.[3] Terror seems to lurk underneath the most ordinary routines of daily life, sometimes erupting on the face of a stranger in the middle of a crowded street. Everything threatens to become utterly bewildering as Malte's consciousness is invaded by the noxious, miserable glee of the people around him: "I felt that the air had long been exhausted, and that I was now breathing only exhaled breath, which my lungs refused."[4] It resembles a scene out of Sartre's *Nausea*, as Rilke explores an unbearable condition for which no effective remedy can be found—at least, not at this point in his career.

In another well-known prose work, *Letters to a Young Poet*, Rilke writes memorably to his correspondent about the anxieties of life, the paradoxes of love, the importance of solitude and self-trust, and the dangers of thoughtless conformity in a world that is "filled with

3 Rilke, *The Notebooks of Malte Laurids Brigge*, trans. by M. D. Herter Norton (New York: W. W. Norton, 1964), 194.

4 *The Notebooks of Malte Laurids Brigge*, 49.

hostility toward the individual, saturated as it were with the hatred of those who find themselves mute and sullen in an insipid duty."[5] The inward dictates of conscience have a sacred authority, Rilke insists, as opposed to the forces that would pull us into an existence that is not our own. So easily, he avows, we can slip back from all that we've labored to attain, falling into a life we never intended:

> can find that we are trapped, as in a dream,
> and die there, without ever waking up.
> This can happen.[6]

Such intimate terms of address will be familiar to readers of Kierkegaard and Nietzsche, and it is no surprise that those who are moved by the writings of these nineteenth-century thinkers have often responded favorably to Rilke as well. Against the philosophical ideal of impersonal knowledge, both Kierkegaard and Nietzsche view philosophy as a creative art, a literary vocation in which all facets of the author's personality are involved. In seeking to develop a mode of reflective writing that would speak to the predicament of the individual, each of these pioneers of existential thought was feverishly devoted to his intellectual mission. In different ways,

5   Letter of 23 December 1903 to Franz X. Kappus, in *Letters to a Young Poet*, trans. by Stephen Mitchell (New York: Vintage, 1986), 57.

6   From "Requiem for a Friend," in *The Selected Poetry of Rainer Maria Rilke*, ed. and trans. by Stephen Mitchell (New York: Vintage, 1989), 85. Other than altering the last word of this passage from "occur" to "happen," I have used Mitchell's translation. Other references to this edition will use Mitchell's versions unless otherwise indicated.

Kierkegaard and Nietzsche found themselves possessed with a sense of necessity, claiming that their work was driven by an unbidden inspiration.[7] This seems to be consistent with Rilke's own experience of the creative process, and with his conception of the author's task: as Harold Bloom notes, "any investigation of the phenomenon of literary genius ought to include Rilke, whose major elegies and sonnets resulted from . . . visitations that he himself regarded as transcendental breakthroughs."[8] However, this sincere faith in the writer's vocation is only one bit of the shared terrain between Rilke and his precursors.

In 1904, Rilke traveled to Copenhagen and (independently) began to discover Kierkegaard's pseudonymous writings and his letters to his fiancée Regine Olsen.[9] He was fascinated by much of what he found in these works, including but not limited to "the Kierkegaardian

7 See, e.g., Kierkegaard's remark that being an author is "not voluntary; on the contrary, it is in line with everything in my personality and its deepest urge." From Søren Kierkegaard, *Journals and Papers: A Selection*, trans. by Alastair Hannay (London: Penguin, 1996), 244. See also Nietzsche's claims about inspiration in *Ecce Homo*, trans. by R. J. Hollingdale (London: Penguin, 1992), 72: "One is merely [the] medium of overwhelming forces. . . . One hears, one does not seek; one takes, one does not ask who gives; a thought flashes up like lightning, with necessity, unfalteringly formed—I have never had any choice."

8 *Genius* (New York: Warner Books, 2002), 720. Rilke's own letters attest to his belief in "character, fate, genius, calling, daimon, soul, destiny," or whatever other name it may be given: see James Hillman, *The Soul's Code* (New York: Warner Books, 1997), 10.

9 See Wolfgang Leppmann, *Rilke: A Life*, trans. by Russell Stockman (New York: Fromm, 1984), 193–201.

concern [for] the untranslatable uniqueness of each individual person."[10] Rilke's comments on subjectivity and inwardness have a distinctively Kierkegaardian ring to them, as do his critique of mass society and his account of why it is essential to preserve the memory of those whom we have loved and who have passed away.[11] And although Rilke's acquaintance with Nietzsche's books may have been limited, his close relationship with Lou Andreas-Salomé gave Rilke the opportunity to learn about Nietzsche's ideas from someone who had not only written a book about the philosopher but had notoriously spent a year of intense companionship with him earlier in her life.[12] We can hear echoes of Nietzsche's *Zarathustra* when Rilke espouses the value of creative striving over mundane contentment, and in his statement that poets as well as philosophers must look

10   Timothy Clark, *The Poetics of Singularity* (Edinburgh: Edinburgh University Press, 2005), 159–60. Cf. Siegfried Mandel, *Rainer Maria Rilke: The Poetic Instinct* (Carbondale: Southern Illinois University Press, 1965), 78.

11   See his letter of 23 September 1908 to Elisabeth Schenk zu Schweinsberg, in *The Poet's Guide to Life: The Wisdom of Rilke*, ed. and trans. by Ulrich Baer (New York: Modern Library, 2005), 107. Cf. David Kleinbard, *The Beginning of Terror: A Psychological Study of Rainer Maria Rilke's Life and Work* (New York and London: New York University Press, 1993), 158–59. For Kierkegaard's discourse on this subject, see "The Work of Love in Recollecting One Who Is Dead," in *Works of Love*, trans. by Howard and Edna Hong (Princeton, NJ: Princeton University Press, 1995), 345–58.

12   This explanation of how Rilke is likely to have learned about Nietzsche, although somewhat speculative, seems to be accepted by many scholars: see Leppmann, *Rilke: A Life*, 79 and Kleinbard, *The Beginning of Terror*, 52.

to the future for their audience.[13] Moreover, a Nietzschean theme that recurs throughout Rilke's poetry (as we shall see) is the love of what is inevitable, as shown in the attitude we adopt when "we most passionately, most tremblingly affirm our being-here, [and] all that happens."[14]

Although Rilke was familiar with the writings of Fyodor Dostoevsky and Herman Hesse, both of whom are key figures in the existential tradition, the other author whose work is most directly pertinent to Rilke's poetry is Martin Heidegger, who was fourteen years younger than Rilke and outlived him by five decades. It is difficult to tell how much Rilke's writings might have directly influenced Heidegger, but the parallels between the two thinkers are striking. According to Heidegger, we live in a "destitute" time, one in which the divine radiance of things is hidden; for this reason, we are in need of poets who can bring the world back to life so that it is once again weighted with significance.[15] In the essay where he articulates this idea, Heidegger locates one source of disenchantment in the

13 Letter of 28 July 1901 to Alexander Benois, in *The Poet's Guide to Life: The Wisdom of Rilke*, 139. Cf. Friedrich Nietzsche, *Thus Spoke Zarathustra*, trans. by Walter Kaufmann (New York: Penguin Books, 1966), 325–27.

14 Rilke, letter of 6 January 1923 to Margot Sizzo, in *The Poet's Guide to Life: The Wisdom of Rilke*, 112. For Nietzsche's portrayal of *amor fati*, the state in which one "wants nothing to be other than it is," see *Ecce Homo*, 37.

15 Heidegger, "What Are Poets For?," in *Poetry, Language, Thought*, trans. by Albert Hofstadter (New York: Harper & Row, 1971), 94–111. See also Julian Young, *Heidegger's Philosophy of Art* (Cambridge: Cambridge University Press, 2001), 95, 144–47.

nihilistic reign of technology, and he cites Rilke in support of his argument. Writing in 1925 to his Polish translator, Rilke laments that his generation may be the last to have known a real world animated with meaning—that is, before empty, indifferent, and fraudulent contrivances started to dominate our existence. Not that there is anything intrinsically wrong with artifice or technology: the techniques of the artist, rightly understood, provide a mode of access to the truth about reality.[16] Nonetheless, technical inventiveness is seldom oriented by such noble aims in a culture dominated by science. Since the prevailing bias is to regard quantitative measurement as the only legitimate route to knowledge, our world of color, sound, and emotion is undermined by the notion that what truly exists is nothing but dull matter. By contrast, the poet employs a different method of "taking measure," abiding by the insight that real qualitative features of the world may be revealed through our affective experience.[17] Poetry can redeem life by illuminating an aspect of things that is concealed from the scientist's view. This delivers us back to a world that is fit to be inhabited by human beings, in which meaning has

16   Heidegger, *The Question Concerning Technology*, trans. by William Lovitt (New York: Harper & Row, 1977), 12–13.

17   See *Poetry, Language, Thought*, 24–25, 219–21. On the way that poetry can enable us to see things "as they are anew, under a new aspect, transfigured, subject to a felt variation," see Simon Critchley, *Things Merely Are* (London and New York: Routledge, 2005), 10–12.

once again become apparent.[18] As our sense of reality expands, our emotional awareness is refined. The poet's goal, then, is not to escape from hard reality into some fantasy of his or her own invention; it is to transform and amplify whatever is there to be perceived, opening up new worlds of tangible value rather than merely neutral facts.

Poetic revelation occurs whenever something is uncovered and brought to light by the literary work of art. The poem is the incarnation of a certain way of seeing things, one "which emphasizes their emotive coloration" or, one might say, their affective significance.[19] This attention to concrete reality is a central motif in Rilke's *Duino Elegies*, the series of poems he completed along with the *Sonnets to Orpheus* in February 1922—and which is closely related in spirit to the latter work. The First Elegy presents everyday phenomena as beckoning toward us to be appreciated and even transformed through the radiant gaze of the receptive subject. "If your everyday life seems poor," Rilke says, "don't blame *it*; blame yourself; admit to yourself that you are not enough of a poet to call forth its riches."[20]

18   Poetry "makes beings more meaningful," as Heidegger states in *The Essence of Truth*, trans. by Ted Sadler (London: Continuum, 2002), 47. On the role played by the imagination in "the disclosure of reality or truth," see Colin Falck, *Myth, Truth, and Literature* (Cambridge: Cambridge University Press, 1989), 138.

19   Maurice Natanson, *The Erotic Bird: Phenomenology in Literature* (Princeton, NJ: Princeton University Press, 1998), 8–9. As Rilke says in a letter of 9 March 1899 to Elena Woronina, "Seeing is for us the most authentic possibility of acquiring something." From *The Poet's Guide to Life: The Wisdom of Rilke*, 8.

20   Letter of 17 February 1903 to Franz X. Kappus, in *Letters to a Young Poet*, 7–8. Or, as he explains in a letter of 8 December 1911 to Sidonie Nádherny von Borutin:

When tree, jug, and flower are acknowledged in the song of the poet, they come to exist in the inward space of experience, thus taking on a higher degree of actuality, becoming "more truthful and more real than they otherwise might be."[21] The most emphatic variety of this acknowledgment is wholehearted celebration or praise. For Rilke, this above all is the poet's essential duty: "endless affirmation and always more affirmation of existence."[22] His poetry alludes to a state of being in which one wishes that everything be just the way it is — as a result, "existence is still enchanted and sacred,"[23] and life is worth living.

Of course, no affirmation of existence can be convincing unless it takes into account what is most horrifying: "just as the artist may not choose what he wants to behold," or see only what he wants to see, he

---

"The possibility of intensifying things so that they reveal their essence depends so much on our participation." From *The Poet's Guide to Life: The Wisdom of Rilke*, 22.

21   Lou Andreas-Salomé, *You Alone Are Real to Me: Remembering Rainer Maria Rilke*, trans. by Angela von der Lippe (Rochester, NY: BOA Editions, 2003), 95. Merleau-Ponty ascribes to art the role of "bringing truth into being." See *The Phenomenology of Perception*, trans. by Colin Smith (New York: Routledge, 2002), xxiii. Heidegger's indebtedness to Rilke in developing this idea is addressed by Michael Zimmerman in *Heidegger's Confrontation with Modernity* (Bloomington: Indiana University Press, 1990), 237–41.

22   Letter of 13 March 1920 to Rudolf Bodländer, in *The Poet's Guide to Life: The Wisdom of Rilke*, 59.

23   Paul Ricoeur, *Freedom and Nature*, 475.

also "may not turn his gaze away from any form of existence."[24] This means that the poet must come to terms with all of the disagreeable features of human life, not least of which is the fragility and impermanence of all things. In a life of tragic suffering and loss, Rilke suggests, we find ourselves forever taking leave, eventually departing from life itself. Rather than taking comfort in an evasion of this fact, or raging against it, Rilke attempts to make "an affirmation of the entire process that leads over and over again to death."[25] The finality of death must somehow be accommodated within any celebratory stance. What we see when we view things charitably differs from what we notice when we come looking for something to find fault with or to condemn.[26] In the Fourth Elegy, Rilke puts forward the thought that it might be a rare achievement to find beauty in human life while recognizing that it is finite.

Life can be affirmed whether or not it is worth affirming; to speak in praise of being is not to assert that such praise is objectively warranted. The undertones of grief and lamentation are always present

24   Rilke, letter of 19 October 1907 to Clara Rilke, in *The Poet's Guide to Life: The Wisdom of Rilke*, 148–49.

25   Richard Detsch, *Rilke's Connections to Nietzsche* (Lanham, MD: University Press of America, 2003), 96. See also Donald A. Prater, *A Ringing Glass: The Life of Rainer Maria Rilke* (New York: Oxford University Press, 1986), 353–54.

26   Cf. M. Jamie Ferreira, *Love's Grateful Striving* (Oxford: Oxford University Press, 2001), 105; she acknowledges Kierkegaard as the source of this idea. In a related vein, Louis Zukofsky notes that "only love looking with the eyes has perfect taste." This is from his *Bottom: On Shakespeare* (Berkeley and Los Angeles: University of California Press, 1987), 19.

in Rilke's poetry: the reader is "never given the impression that an optimist is speaking."[27] The reason for adopting a positive attitude toward existence despite all of its miseries and limitations is "*not* because happiness *exists*," but "because *truly* being here is so much," and

> everything here
> apparently needs us, this fleeting world, which in some strange way
> keeps calling to us. Us, the most fleeting of all.[28]

Like Kierkegaard, Rilke believes that gratitude for life must take the form of unconditional acceptance.[29] "Joy," he claims, is categorically "more than happiness," for "happiness befalls people, happiness is

---

27 Heinz F. Peters, *Rainer Maria Rilke: Masks and the Man* (Seattle: University of Washington Press, 1960), 177–78. In a letter of 6 January 1923 to Margot Sizzo, Rilke considers that perhaps we should not "desire consolation over a loss," but "experience the peculiarity, the singularity, and the effects of *this* loss in our life," so that "its significance and weight" might "enrich our inner world." From *The Poet's Guide to Life: The Wisdom of Rilke*, 109.

28 From "The Ninth Elegy," in *The Selected Poetry of Rainer Maria Rilke*, 199. On the foolishness of our usual assumptions about where "happiness" might be found, when "it really isn't at all important to be happy" in any case, see Rilke's letter of 17 August 1901 to Emanuel von Bodman, in *Rilke on Love and Other Difficulties*, trans. by John Mood (New York: W. W. Norton, 1993), 27.

29 See my treatment of this theme in Furtak, *Wisdom in Love: Kierkegaard and the Ancient Quest for Emotional Integrity* (Notre Dame, IN: University of Notre Dame Press, 2005), 112–14.

fate, while people cause joy to bloom inside themselves."[30] This is a gratuitous state of mind, not justified by any evidence; and yet, some properties of the world would be lost on us in its absence. Just as the blind person knows nothing about colors, the person who has not adopted the poet's "lyrical way of experiencing the world" is not fully aware of the meaning and value of things.[31] In order to discern these qualities in our environment, we must have the right kind of receptivity. What is at stake here is "the birth of sense (or significance) itself," the subjective conditions that allow for the world's emergence and realization.[32]

This explains Rilke's continuing emphasis on "learning to see," and on striving to become more mindful and less oblivious toward the intricate reality that surrounds us. Although his narrator Malte, in the *Notebooks*, ultimately fails to approach the world with a spirit

30   Letter of 5 December 1914 to Marianne von Goldschmidt-Rothschild, in *The Poet's Guide to Life: The Wisdom of Rilke*, 175. Cf. Clément Rosset, *Joyful Cruelty*, ed. and trans. by David F. Bell (New York: Oxford University Press, 1993), 17: "Either joy consists of an ephemeral illusion of having gotten rid of the tragic nature of existence . . . or it consists of an approbation of existence which is held to be irremediably tragic, in which case joy is paradoxical, but it is not illusory."

31   Leppmann, *Rilke: A Life*, 55. See also Priscilla Washburn Shaw, *Rilke, Valéry and Yeats: The Domain of the Self* (New Brunswick: Rutgers University Press, 1964), 76–77: on "revelation" as "experiencing fully the reality and variety of the world."

32   John Lysaker, *You Must Change Your Life: Poetry, Philosophy, and the Birth of Sense* (University Park: Penn State University Press, 2002), 55. Likewise, springtime is not just an event that occurs in the nonhuman universe, since it "requires the feelings appropriate to it" in order to "come into its own." See Konstantin Kolenda, "Immortality Revisited," *Philosophy and Literature* 4 (1980): 169.

of passionate acceptance, Rilke himself in a 1914 poem records the observation that this "world that is looked at so deeply / wants to flourish in love."[33] As another poet has pointed out, "the primary experience of perception" is shaped by "what the artist believes to be the qualitative nature of the things perceived."[34] When the poet "opens up to receive, in a flood of emotion, the being of the thing he sees," then he or she has arrived at the "way of seeing things" which is "the origin of poetry."[35] When I am in love with someone, I am able to appreciate her best qualities, because these are enhanced in the light of my affirmative gaze. The obligation that weighs on Rilke's Orphic poet is to extend this outlook more broadly, so that all of existence is encompassed in a song of nonpossessive love, an anthem of unqualified praise.

33 From "Turning-Point," in *The Selected Poetry of Rainer Maria Rilke*, 135. Malte's hope that he is "learning to see" is recorded in *The Notebooks of Malte Laurids Brigge*, 14. Rilke's indictment of this work's failings can be found in his letter of 8 November 1915 to Lotte Hepner, in *The Poet's Guide to Life: The Wisdom of Rilke*, 18–19.

34 Kathleen Raine, *Defending Ancient Springs* (New York: Oxford University Press, 1967), 114. Echoing Heidegger, J. Glenn Gray points out that human experience will be impoverished unless we "become aware that the poetic eye is capable of seeing as deeply . . . as the scientific eye." See "Poets and Thinkers," in *Phenomenology and Existentialism*, ed. by Edward N. Lee and Maurice Mandelbaum (Baltimore: Johns Hopkins University Press, 1967), 107.

35 J. Hillis Miller, *The Disappearance of God* (Urbana: University of Illinois Press, 2000), 321.

Anxiously we grapple for a hold—
sometimes, we're too young for what is old
and too old for that which never was.

Still, it's only fair to praise, because:
oh, nonetheless.[36]

By now it ought to be clear that basic questions about the human condition can be explored in poetry, just as they can be explored in more traditional philosophical texts.[37] Others have already surmised that the existential philosopher's role may be to "*describe* the world in such a way that its meanings emerge," and that this job is perhaps best accomplished by more literary modes of writing.[38] The poet's appeal to human emotions, and his or her attention to concrete particulars, can no longer be seen as grounds for banishment from the ideal republic. According to Merleau-Ponty, even for philosophers it is not enough "to create or express an idea; they must also awaken the experiences which will make their idea take root in the

36 From *Sonnets to Orpheus*, 2.23 (my translation). All direct citations of this work will be my own translation unless otherwise indicated. On "praise" as the appropriate response to "the monstrosities" and "the nameless grays," see the untitled 1921 poem written as an inscription in one of Rilke's books: *Rilke on Love and Other Difficulties*, 65; and Prater, *A Ringing Glass*, 351.

37 See Lysaker, *You Must Change Your Life*, 12. Falck conjectures that "lyric poetry might be thought of as the most essential of our linguistic modes of apprehension of reality." See *Myth, Truth, and Literature*, 60.

38 Mary Warnock, *Existentialism* (Oxford: Oxford University Press, 1970), 136; see also Kaufmann, *Existentialism from Dostoevsky to Sartre*, 49.

consciousness of others."[39] If this is true, and "axioms in philosophy are not axioms until they are proved upon our pulses,"[40] then some poetic skill might be precisely what is required in order to bring an idea home to one's readers in a compelling way.

And yet: there is more to be said about poetry, beyond the fact that it can manifest an attitude or bring home an idea. If Rilke simply wanted to tell a story or make an argument, then he might just as well be writing novels or essays instead of poems. Because he is composing poetry in a highly formal mode, Rilke is also calling our attention to the music of words, regardless of whatever else he is doing. In poetry, language is never merely a means to reaching an end outside the poem itself. Whatever the narrative and propositional content of a poem might be, an unpoetic summary of this content would not exhaustively capture what is going on in the actual poem. In the Seventh Elegy, when Rilke exclaims that "*truly being here is glorious,*"[41] this might sound like any other declarative statement—except that it is located in the midst of a poem, which is not only making sense but also sounding.[42] Since both sound and

39   *Sense and Non-Sense*, trans. by Hubert L. and Patricia Dreyfus (Evanston, IL: Northwestern University Press, 1964), 19.

40   John Keats, letter of 3 May 1818 to J. H. Reynolds, in *Letters of John Keats*, ed. Robert Gittings (Oxford: Oxford University Press, 1970), 93.

41   See *The Selected Poetry of Rainer Maria Rilke*, 189.

42   Poetry is made of words, and words "are, in poetry, sounds." See Wallace Stevens, "The Noble Rider and the Sound of Words," in *The Necessary Angel* (New York: Vintage, 1951), 32. This is why Martha Nussbaum brackets lyric poetry as

sense "demand a great deal of attention," as readers we must attend simultaneously to two aspects of a poem that exist in tension with one another.[43] When a poet makes assertions or defends abstract ideas in verse, he or she cannot prevent "the attention given to following the ideas from competing with the attention that follows the song."[44] For this reason, the didactic poetry of Lucretius is at odds with the nature of things. Still, in the free stanzas of the *Duino Elegies*, ideas seem to take the lead while sound recedes into the background. In the *Sonnets to Orpheus*, however, the musical properties of Rilke's language are too prominent to ignore: this sequence of poems might be described as formally "dense" due to its metrical and repetitive structure.[45] It is therefore problematic to read these sonnets as any-

---

raising "different issues" than fiction: *Love's Knowledge* (Oxford: Oxford University Press, 1990), 46.

43   Amittai Aviram, *Telling Rhythm* (Ann Arbor: University of Michigan Press, 1994), 50. On the "quite distinct" ways of thinking associated with poetry and philosophy, see John Koethe, "Thought and Poetry," *Midwest Studies in Philosophy* 25 (2001): 5.

44   Paul Valéry, *The Art of Poetry*, trans. by Denise Folliot (Princeton, NJ: Princeton University Press, 1958), 77–78. The other side of the story, as Michael Hamburger observes, is that "words can never be totally severed from the connection with ideas and meaning." See his *The Truth of Poetry* (New York: Harcourt Brace, 1970), 38. This is why, even when it "privileges the phonic over the semantic function of language," Rilke's poetry is not a "sheer play of signifiers," as Véronique Fóti shows in *Heidegger and the Poets* (Atlantic Highlands, NJ: Humanities Press, 1992), 38–39.

45   Cf. Anna Christina Ribeiro, "Intending to Repeat: A Definition of Poetry," *Journal of Aesthetics and Art Criticism* 65 (2007): 191.

thing other than poetry—to reduce them to their conceptual content, for instance, as a philosopher might be inclined to do.

Through their exemplary resistance to paraphrase, Rilke's sonnets serve as a reminder that poetry cannot be assimilated to any other genre of writing in which the sound of words does not command notice in the same way. This ought to be welcomed by those readers "who love poetry for its own sake," as Auden says, rather than because a poem gives voice to feelings or beliefs they happen to endorse.[46] Through its pitch, rhythm, and tone, poetry approaches the art of music as a kind of upper limit, to appropriate Zukofsky's apt definition.[47] It would be a mistake to dismiss the metrical elements of a poem as primitive efforts at articulating something that could be expressed equally well in flat prosaic speech. The cadences of words and phrases, the sound of vowels and staccato of consonants, and the rhyme scheme of the lines combine to highlight the physical texture

46   W. H. Auden, "Introduction" to Shakespeare's *Sonnets*, ed. by William Burto (New York: Signet Classics, 1964), xvii. Similar comments are made by A. E. Housman, in *The Name and Nature of Poetry* (Cambridge: Cambridge University Press, 1933), 33–34: "Most readers, when they think they are admiring poetry, are really admiring, not the poetry [itself] . . . but something else in it, which they like better than poetry."

47   Louis Zukofsky, "A Statement for Poetry," in *Prepositions: The Collected Critical Essays* (Middletown, CT: Wesleyan University Press, 2000), 19. This stands in contrast to the position of Yvor Winters, who contends that a good poem ought to make "a defensible rational statement." See *In Defense of Reason* (Athens, OH: Swallow / Ohio University Press, 1947), 11.

of words as distinguished from the meaning conveyed.[48] However, this does not necessarily frustrate the poem's truth-disclosing function. There are several reasons for this.

Lyric poetry's dependence on the spirit of music, noted by Nietzsche in *The Birth of Tragedy*, implies that the language of a poem has sonic *as well as* semantic force.[49] The one does not obliterate the other, since both are present at once. There is an impression made by the pattern of sounds in a poem, however elusive it may seem when we try to describe the significance of what has been impressed upon us. It is by no means farfetched to conclude that there is a relation "between certain types of tonal gesturing and certain types of attitude."[50] For the sound of a poem can intimate a state of mind, over and above whatever thoughts it also contains. This is one reason why it would be unwise "to dismiss this concern for attractive sur-

---

48   See H. P. Rickman, *Philosophy in Literature* (London: Associated University Presses, 1996), 26. The materiality of language may be part of what Michel de Certeau has in mind when he calls mystical writing a "manner of speaking" that seeks "experimental knowledge" which is *founded* in being, rather than *adequate* to being. What emerges in the words of a poem, then, has a reality of its own in addition to whatever present reality is denoted by those words. See *The Mystic Fable*, trans. by Michael Smith (Chicago: University of Chicago Press, 1992), 113–45.

49   Nietzsche, *The Birth of Tragedy*, trans. by William A. Haussmann (New York: Barnes and Noble, 2006), 22.

50   Kenneth Burke, *The Philosophy of Literary Form* (New York: Vintage, 1957), 303. For Kathleen Raine, the music of a poem "communicates a meaning and a knowledge not of fact but of quality." See *Defending Ancient Springs*, 175.

faces all too hastily as a form of aestheticism."[51] But that is not all: as Rilke cryptically says in a letter, rhyme is "the deity of very secret and very ancient coincidences."[52] The random fact that some words sound alike is a happy coincidence, from which many insights can be gathered. By concentrating on the technical demands of meter and rhyme, the poet who composes a sonnet is liable to think of possible formulations that would not have occurred to him or her otherwise.[53] For Rilke, the process of composition involves more receptivity than deliberate control, and its fruits are experienced as a gift that could not have been anticipated. Lacking the freedom to write down the first things that come to mind, he is forced to go beyond what he was already prepared to say.

In this way, formal constraint can actually be liberating, since it provokes a poet to discover combinations of words that reveal

---

51 Paul de Man, *Allegories of Reading* (New Haven, CT: Yale University Press, 1979), 22–23. In our engagement with a poem, John Lysaker writes, "content is not given to us mentally while our senses remain afloat upon a sea of *aisthesis*." See *You Must Change Your Life*, 8.

52 Letter of 23 March 1921 to Rolf von Ungern-Sternberg, in *The Poet's Guide to Life: The Wisdom of Rilke*, 130.

53 Cf. William Stafford, "A Way of Writing," in *Writing the Australian Crawl* (Ann Arbor: University of Michigan Press, 1978), 17. The "gift" that is at issue here merits comparison with Jean-Luc Marion's notion of "The Saturated Phenomenon," as presented in *Phenomenology and the "Theological Turn,"* ed. by Dominique Janicaud (New York: Fordham University Press, 2000), 185–99.

something that he or she did not already know.[54] Whether sacred or profane, audible language can bring about a genuine revelation, leading us to arrive at unpredictable insights that are utterly new to us. Sometimes, what gets turned up by this process is a phrase that is suggestive but opaque: "The fact is the sweetest dream that labor knows."[55] Yet a precise, compact line may express a truth that escapes being contained in a more prosaic statement, especially when there is no plain statement to be made about the matter at hand. Just when we think we have arrived at the edge of the ineffable, our formal method allows us to say *something* rather than nothing, extending the range of what can be revealed through language.[56] When a poet gives voice with formal precision to an uncertain state of mind, he or she allows what was previously undisclosed to come forth.

---

54   On this topic see H. L. Hix, "Formal Experimentation and Poetic Discovery," in *As Easy as Lying: Essays on Poetry* (Silver Spring, MD: Etruscan Press, 2002), 50–56. See also P. Christopher Smith, "A Poem of Rilke: Evidence for the Later Heidegger," *Philosophy Today* 21 (1977): 254.

55   Line 13 of Robert Frost's sonnet "Mowing," in *The Poetry of Robert Frost*, ed. by Edward Connery Lathem (New York: Henry Holt and Company, 1979), 17. Arthur Schopenhauer points out that rhyme lends a sense of inevitability to whatever is said in a poem: see *The World as Will and Representation, Volume Two*, trans. by E. F. J. Payne (New York: Dover, 1966), 428–29.

56   Christian Wiman writes that "there are effects available to traditionally formal poems which aren't available to other poems," one of which "has to do with an intensification of the uncertainty and even open-endedness that we normally associate with looser forms." See his essay "An Idea of Order," in *After New Formalism: Poets on Form, Narrative, and Tradition*, ed. by Annie Finch (Ashland, OR: Story Line Press, 1999), 210. See also Aviram, *Telling Rhythm*, 233.

This duality of sense and sound poses a special challenge for the translator of poetry. Since the primary goal of a poem is not to transmit information, it is not enough to jump from one dictionary to another and construct a literal equivalent of the original: instead, it is necessary to remake the poem *as* a poem in the target language. If the original poem is not merely saying things, but also *doing* things with words, then a version of this poem in a different language should do the same kind of thing. This means that the translator of Rilke must strive to do justice to the sonic achievement of the original, not losing touch with either Rilke's meaning or *how* it is meant.[57] These twin exigencies compel the translator poet to be a copyist and an original artist at the same time. Poetic translation is a kind of writing, and the translator of poetry has to be a poet while translating regardless of whether or not he or she also writes poetry of his or her own.[58] An adequate translation of a prose work might preclude any further translations of the same text, at least for a while. However, no one would call a poem "adequate" except to condemn it with faint praise — and this applies just as well to poetry in translation. Therefore, no translated poem could be so perfect as to render superfluous all fur-

---

57   On "what is meant" and "the way of meaning it," see Walter Benjamin, "The Task of the Translator," in *Selected Writings: Volume One*, ed. by Michael W. Jennings and Marcus Bullock (Cambridge, MA: Harvard University Press, 1996), 257. As Nelson Goodman notes of art in general, "we cannot merely look through the symbol to what it refers to"; rather, we must attend "to the symbol itself." See *Ways of Worldmaking* (Hassocks, UK: Harvester Press, 1978), 69.

58   See, e.g., Willis Barnstone, *The Poetics of Translation: History, Theory, Practice* (New Haven, CT: Yale University Press, 1993), 7–8, 270.

ther attempts to do in English something like what Rilke has done in German. Ricoeur is probably right when he cites "dissatisfaction with regard to existing translations" as the chief motive for retranslating;[59] when Wyatt and Surrey each created English versions of the same Petrarch sonnet, they inaugurated a long and ongoing tradition of admirable failures to do the impossible.

Nevertheless, some attempts are better than others. The *Sonnets to Orpheus* are profoundly shaped by the auditory, as opposed to the visual, imagination; they are held together by patterns of assonance that call to each other even between the end rhymes that recur throughout the sequence.[60] The obsessive and repetitious rhythms of the sonnets serve to induce a state of trancelike, heightened inwardness. Their musicality reminds us that, just as poetic language is "more than a vehicle for the transmission of axioms and concepts," so also rhythm is "more than a physiological motor. It is capable

59   Paul Ricoeur, *On Translation*, trans. by Eileen Brennan (London: Routledge, 2006), 7. One of the defects of poetic translation that is "formally vague" and "stylistically impoverished," according to Dana Gioia, is that "unrhymed, unmetered and unshaped, Petrarch and Rilke sound misleadingly alike." From *Can Poetry Matter?* (Saint Paul, MN: Graywolf Press, 1992), 38.

60   On T. S. Eliot's phrase "auditory imagination," which denotes "the feeling for syllable and rhythm," see Adam Piette, *Remembering and the Sound of Words* (New York: Oxford University Press, 1996), 148–49. Cf. Eliot, "The Music of Poetry," in *On Poetry and Poets* (London: Faber and Faber, 1957), 30: "If we are moved by a poem, it has meant something, perhaps something important, to us; if we are not moved, then it is, as poetry, meaningless."

of registering . . . deep shocks of recognition."[61] Such effects com-
municate intense feeling and conviction in a way that is only dissi-
pated by the diffuse style of less orderly poems.[62] And yet the readers
of some Rilke translations would be astounded to learn about this.
Frequently, Anglophone translators of Rilke have assumed that read-
ers do not need to experience anything like the texture and form of
the original and that these can be safely be left out of the English
adaptation.

For instance, William Gass and Robert Bly are well-known con-
temporary authors who have ventured to translate a few of the *Sonnets
to Orpheus* (approximately ten apiece, out of the total—fifty-five)
while commenting on how the poems ought to be translated. Not
only do both of them make scant use of rhyme and regular meter, but
they also volunteer their own scornful and dismissive views of metri-
cal form. Gass takes the second poem (1.02) and warps its rhymed

---

61 Geoffrey Hill, *The Lords of Limit: Essays on Literature and Ideas* (Oxford: Oxford
University Press, 1984), 87. On "inwardness" in Rilke, see Hans Egon Holthusen,
Rainer Maria Rilke: A Study of His Later Work (New Haven, CT: Yale University
Press, 1952), 11.

62 Cf. Louis Mackey, *Kierkegaard: A Kind of Poet* (Philadelphia: University of
Pennsylvania Press, 1971), 267. Samuel Taylor Coleridge calls for "a more than
usual state of emotion" to be combined in a poet with "more than usual order"
in *Biographia Literaria*, ed. by Nigel Leask (London: Everyman, 1997), 185. See
also Anthony Storr, *Music and the Mind* (New York: Ballantine Books, 1992), 103:
"Those who are especially threatened by disorder are those most strongly motivated
to discover order." Timothy Steele makes a similar claim during an interview with
William Baer, in *Formalist* 14 (2003): 28–29.

pentameter sestet into seven irregular lines of free verse, ranging from five to twelve syllables in length, while patting himself on the back for rendering the poem "as the poet wrote it."[63] As for Bly, who also scoffs at formal poetry in general and at the sonnet in particular, he expands the phrase *Gesang ist Dasein* from the third poem in Rilke's sequence (1.03) from three words to seven, converting it from a compact aphorism into an ordinary-language paraphrase: "to write poetry is to be alive."[64] These results are typical. When translators of the *Sonnets to Orpheus* assume that it would be idolatrous to insist on using a sonnet-like meter and rhyme, the outcome is a greater sacrilege.[65] Having noticed this kind of discrepancy, but being unable

63   William H. Gass, *Reading Rilke: Reflections on the Problems of Translation* (New York: Knopf, 1999), 84–85. His snide comments on the sonnet form can be found on page 52; for some of his cheap shots at Rilke's "alleged ideas," see pages 32–33. *Ad hominem* attacks on Rilke himself can be found throughout: I agree entirely with J. M. Coetzee that Gass manages to convey the patronizing attitude that, "compared with William Gass, Rilke was a bit of a fool, a bit of a booby." See *Stranger Shores* (New York: Penguin, 2002), 64–65.

64   From *Selected Poems of Rainer Maria Rilke*, trans. by Robert Bly (New York: Harper & Row, 1981), 198–99. This case calls to mind William Logan's remarks on a "Shakespeare Online" rendition of Sonnet 29, in which "When in disgrace with fortune and men's eyes" has become "When I've run out of luck and people look down on me." See "The Bowl of Diogenes," *Poetry* 187 (2006): 414.

65   Willis Barnstone submits that "if one disapproves of rhyme in poetry," then "one should not translate poems that rhyme." See "Preferences in Translating Poetry," in *Translation*, ed. by William Frawley (Newark, DE: University of Delaware Press, 1984), 50. Those who are made squeamish by talk of reverence and irreverence are unlikely to be the most sympathetic audience for Rilke's work. Yet Leppmann is

to dispense with translations altogether, I started to conceive of an English version that would be similar to Rilke's original text in body and soul.

Since I am not a German scholar, I was encouraged to find one of Rilke's commentators observe that, "in the translation of poetry, even a very *good* acquaintance with the source language is no guarantee of anything."[66] Although expert knowledge of the source language could hardly be counted as a drawback, it might also remove the principal motive for undertaking a translation. Rilke himself, for instance, made a German version of Elizabeth Barrett Browning's *Sonnets from the Portuguese*, in spite of the fact that he knew English about as well as he knew Portuguese — that is, hardly at all.[67] In this respect, Rilke's translators have not hesitated to follow his example. Commenting on several recent editions of Rilke in English, Marjorie Perloff observes with some consternation that "none of the transla-

---

exasperated by Rilke's belief in his poetic vocation; and Don Paterson announces, in commenting on Rilke's sonnets, that he himself is devoutly sure that "faith in *anything* is misplaced." See *Rilke: A Life*, 25; and Paterson, *Orpheus* (London: Faber and Faber, 2006), 79. Rilke himself held that one must believe in poetry in order to write it, seeing the artist as "someone afflicted with an inner mission" and placing trust in this ideal. See his letter of 26 July 1923 to Hans Reinhart, in *The Poet's Guide to Life: The Wisdom of Rilke*, 160. The best way to represent Rilke's poetic faith is through a line by Henry Bugbee, who says: "we must trust in experience that comes to us in the imperative mood." See *Inward Morning* (Athens: University of Georgia Press, 1999), 116.

66 Paterson, *Orpheus*, 82.

67 See Leppmann, *Rilke: A Life*, 226.

tors are themselves bilingual": for instance, one of them admits to possessing "frail German skills," and another claims to read "very little" German.[68] Yet the practice is not so dubious as it may seem. Wishing to create a version of Browning's poems that would sing in his own language, Rilke seems to have been more interested in duplicating the original sonnets' devices of rhyme and alliteration than in reproducing every detail of their literal sense.[69] In dealing with poetry written in an intricate fixed form, it is especially important for the translator to avoid committing the heresy of paraphrase. Because of the sonnet's formal limitations, what is especially challenging about the translator's task is not developing a sense of what is going on in the original. Rather, it is the step that comes *after* one has developed a sense of the original and is now trying to compose something akin to the same poem in a different language. The most highly fluent translator will have an easier time getting at the literal

68   Marjorie Perloff, "Reading Gass Reading Rilke," *Parnassus* 25 (2001) 486–89. Rilke translators are not the only ones to share this belief, either: Jerome Rothenberg, the distinguished translator of world poetry from many languages, confesses that his "grasp of any language other than English has been limited" throughout his career. See his *Writing Through: Translations and Variations* (Middletown, CT: Wesleyan University Press, 2004), xv.

69   Prater, *A Ringing Glass*, 144. Obviously, Rilke did not accept the dogma that a poem simply "constitutes a 'statement' of some sort." Cleanth Brooks uses these terms to characterize what he calls "The Heresy of Paraphrase," in *Twentieth-Century Literary Theory*, ed. by Vassilis Lambropoulos and David N. Miller (Albany: State University of New York Press, 1987), 241.

surface meaning of the original poem, but will not necessarily have any advantage when it comes to the more difficult part of the job.

Here, in the *Sonnets to Orpheus*, Rilke adheres to a fairly consistent rhyme scheme, using four rhymes in each octave and two or three per sestet in diverse arrangements. The standard pattern allows for quite a bit of variety within fourteen lines, but Rilke plays more freely with meter and rhythm, making use of several different line lengths (in some cases, within the same poem). I have accordingly used rhyme throughout the sequence, although I have employed what might be called vowel rhyme or assonantal rhyme quite often, and in a few cases have loosened things up further and rhymed every other line ending. On the other hand, I have kept up a roughly iambic meter somewhat more regularly than Rilke himself, and I have attempted to emulate his own fascination with assonance and internal rhyme. Definite descriptions have been substituted for proper names in a small number of poems—for example, "Orpheus" appears as the "Poet," and "der Gott" is "Orpheus" at least once—and I've curtailed some of Rilke's eccentric habits of punctuation, most notably the yoking together of a colon and a dash when either would be sufficient. These deviations notwithstanding, what follows are sonnets nearly equal in shape and meaning to Rilke's original; which is to say that the poems with shorter lines are those that were composed that way, and that the words and phrases in these verses have a firm basis in Rilke's own.

If there is a cast of characters in the *Sonnets to Orpheus*, then Orpheus himself clearly plays the lead role. A legendary early Greek poet-philosopher who might have lived in Thrace even before

27

Homer,[70] Orpheus is also the mythical figure who is said to have made a journey down into the underworld to retrieve his beloved Eurydice. Their tragic story, which is told by Ovid and recounted in one of Rilke's earlier poems, ends with a fateful backward glance.[71] For Rilke, Orpheus is the archetypal poet, the incarnation of the creative impulse, and the thinker who teaches us how to face life and death with wisdom and courage. As for the dancer who is memorialized in at least two of the sonnets (1.25 and 2.18), Vera Ouckama Knoop died at age nineteen of an illness that bore an uncanny resemblance to Rilke's own. He viewed her as a symbol of artistic openness, delicate beauty, and joyful affirmation in the face of adversity.[72] Even though the whole sequence is "for" Vera and "to" Orpheus in some sense, Vera remains mostly offstage and Orpheus is seldom the direct addressee: these poems are not transparently "about" topics in the way that newspaper articles ought to be. Yet many of the *Sonnets to Orpheus* do seem to be speaking *to* someone. They are filled with

70   Cf. Kathleen Freeman, *Ancilla to the Pre-Socratic Philosophers* (Cambridge, MA: Harvard University Press, 1983), 1–7.

71   See Ovid, *Metamorphoses*, trans. by Rolfe Humphries (Bloomington: Indiana University Press, 1955), 234–37. Cf. *The Selected Poetry of Rainer Maria Rilke*, 48–53.

72   Leukemia was the sickness that led to the death of Vera and of Rilke himself, although in his case it went mysteriously undiagnosed until shortly before his death. Vera's mother Gertrud had sent Rilke a copy of her final journals, which made a powerful impression on him, as attested by his letters of 26 November 1921 to Gertrud Ouckama Knoop and of 12 April 1923 to Margot Sizzo, among others. See, e.g., Leppmann, *Rilke: A Life*, 352–56; Kleinbard, *The Beginning of Terror*, 220–22; and Peters, *Rainer Maria Rilke*, 160–62.

imperatives that appear to be aimed at the reader, unless we interpret them as second-person exhortations intended for the poet himself.

Rilke's own favorite sonnet, which he described as the "most valid" poem in the sequence and as the one that "contains all the rest," is the one (2.13) that opens with "Be ahead of all parting," and which includes the following appeal:

> Amid these fading and decaying things,
> be the glass that rings out as it's breaking.[73]

It is a poem of passionate affirmation, in which the story of Orpheus gives rise to a meditation on human mortality. Life as a whole is presented as a complex episode of departure, always charged with the prospect of loss. It is a condition in which nothing can suffice to provide us with lasting fulfillment; and yet we are asked to be grateful toward the source of our being, to embrace the whole ambiguous mystery.[74] This gratitude is not predicated upon a denial of human suffering, either: our life in this world is not an illusion, nor is it a mere prelude to some life beyond in which all doubts will be put to rest. The spiritual attitude endorsed by the poem is one of unconditional acceptance toward a precarious existence that has not been

73   Regarding this poem, and Rilke's opinion of it, see Frank H. Wood, *Rainer Maria Rilke: The Ring of Forms* (Minneapolis: University of Minnesota Press, 1958), 207. See also Geoffrey H. Hartman, *The Unmediated Vision* (New Haven, CT: Yale University Press, 1954), 90–95.

74   Here, I am indebted to William Waters, "Rilke's Imperatives," *Poetics Today* 25 (2004): 718–24. See also Erica Delsandro, "Patient Endurance: Orpheus, Rilke, and Modern Poetry," *Soundings* 88 (2005): 99.

fully understood. In its closing lines, the sonnet ends with a formal resolution that leaves room for uncertainty. It does not give the illusion of having answered an ultimate question that can only be confronted in fear and trembling.[75] In this way, Rilke sounds out an issue that will never be conceptually resolved. By encouraging his reader to look at all of life as if it had already ended, Rilke seems to be winding up to take a final bow. The gesture would be appropriate, since he survived just a few years beyond the publication of this sequence. And it is hard to imagine a more fitting epitaph for Rilke's life and work.

75 Maurice Blanchot speaks about how Rilke elevates uncertainty and anxiety into "the resolution of an exact formulation." See *The Space of Literature*, trans. by Ann Smock (Lincoln: University of Nebraska Press, 1982), 144. The possibility of resolving intellectual or emotional perplexities in a sonnet, as opposed to any other literary genre, is discussed by Paul Oppenheimer in *The Birth of the Modern Mind* (New York: Oxford University Press, 1989), 3–4.

Sonnets to Orpheus

I.OI

A tree rose up. O zenith of arising!
  Sing, Orpheus! The highest in the ear!
And all was still. Yet, even in the silence,
    new things proceeded; hints of change appeared.

Out of the quiet, creatures came to light,
    emerging from both earth and wood, from nest
and hollow: all were hushed, not out of fright,
    nor due to any ruse. They were possessed

with listening. Then howl, cry, and roar
    grew small within their hearts. And where before
there was barely a place for guests to enter,

a hideout harboring all the darkest urges,
    whose entryway was made of shaky birches —
in their hearing, you raised up a temple.

I.02

It was almost a girl who issued out
    from this happy accord of song and lyre
and glowed translucent through her springtime shroud
    and made herself a bed within my ear.

And slept in me. And everything was her sleep:
    the trees that I looked up to, the unhidden
distances, the meadow I could feel,
    and every wonder I myself was given.

She slept the world. Singing god, how then
    did you fulfill her that she never hoped
to be awake? See, she got up and slept.

Where is her death? O, could you still compose
    this theme before your song dissolves itself?
Where does she sink from me? . . . A girl, almost.

1.03

A god can do it. But how, tell me, does
a man follow him through the narrow harp?
His mind is divided. Where two cross at once
    on heart-ways, there's no temple for Apollo.

Song, as you remind us, isn't longing,
    not a plea for some end to be achieved.
Song is existence—easy for a god,
    but when do *we* exist? And when does *he*

circle the earth and stars around our being?
    Not when you're young and in love, even if
your voice erupts in tongues at such a time.

Learn to forget that song—it will decline.
    True singing needs another way to breathe.
A "nothing" breath. A gust of god. A wind.

1.04

O you gentle ones, from time to time
   step directly into the foreign breath;
as it passes your cheeks, let it divide:
      behind it swirls, becoming one again.

You who are blissful, and you the undamaged,
      you who appear where all hearts have their source;
bows made of arrows and targets of arrows,
      even through tears your smile constantly glows.

Don't recoil from suffering: the weight,
      bring it back to the gravity of Earth.
Heavy are the mountains, heavy the seas.

When you were children, you gave root to trees
      that grew unbearably weighty, even at first.
Still, the air . . . still, the open spaces . . .

1.05

E rect no gravestone; only, let the rose
  bloom every year in memory of him.
For this is Orpheus. His metamorph-
     osis is here, in this and that. Admit,

then, of no other name. Once and for all:
     where there is song, it's Orpheus. He comes
and goes. Isn't it something, for a small
     while, if he outlives the flower buds?

He has to vanish so you'll understand!
     Although he dreads that vanishing, and though
his every word exceeds this place and time,

he's there already — where you cannot go.
     The instrument does not constrain his hands,
and as he steps beyond, he toes the line.

1.06

Is he at home here? No, out of both
   regions his extensive nature bloomed.
Able to bend the willow boughs are those
   who have understood the willow's roots.

When you go to bed, leave out no milk
   or bread on the table: this attracts the dead.
But he, the conjuror, invite him in
   underneath the eyelids' gentle red

to mix appearance into all that's seen;
   and let the magic of fumitory and rue
be as real to him as the clearest thing.

Nothing can tarnish this authentic scene;
   whether it be from graves or living-rooms,
let him admire necklace, jug, and ring.

1.07

Praising, that's it! He was meant to praise,
and flowed like ore out of the quiet stone.
His heart—it was an evanescent press
    that made an ageless wine for us alone.

When he's within a sacred instant's grip,
    his voice is never dusty or dried out.
Everything turns to vineyard, turns to grape,
    mellowing in his tender, sentient South.

Neither the growth of mold in royal vaults,
    nor any shadow cast down by the gods,
could ever undercut his songs of praise.

He is the patient herald who remains,
    delivering the most praiseworthy bowls
of fruit to the dead, who lie beyond the door.

1.08

O nly in the realm of praising may Lament
　　drift, nymph of the tearshed-nourished brook,
who oversees our hearts' disheartenment,
　　making our crying strike the very rock

that raises up the altars and the gates.
　　Look—around her silent shoulders comes
the dawning knowledge that she came here late;
　　among the sisters, she is the most young.

Rejoicing *knows*, and Longing has confessed—
　　only Lament still learns; with gentle hands,
she reckons every night the ancient wrong.

But suddenly, impromptu and askance,
　　she holds a constellation of our song
against a sky untroubled by her breath.

I.09

S omeone who's already lifted
his lyre among shades
may regain a premonition
    of endless praise.

Someone who's dined with the dead,
    on poppies of their own,
will never again forget
    the gentlest tone.

Although, to us, reflections often
    dissolve on the water:
know the picture.

Only in another zone
    do voices first grow
kind and persistent.

I.10

You ancient tombs, who never have been lost
    to me, I greet you, feeling warm at heart;
you, through whom the Roman water frolics
    and every day goes wandering like a song.

Or those who are wide open as the eyes
    of a contented shepherd on waking up
—full of quiet and of honeysuckle—
    around which flit ecstatic butterflies.

I welcome all who wrest away from doubt,
    and all who open up their mouths again,
already having sounded silence out.

Do we know what it means or not, my friends?
    The hesitating hour shapes them both
into an echo of the human form.

I.II

Look at the sky. Is not one constellation
named "Rider"? For this earthly pride is all
too oddly marked in us. And there's a neighbor,
who drives and rides and brings it to a halt.

Isn't this being driven and restrained
just like the sinewy nature of our life?
Roadway and turn-off. But a touch explains.
New vast expanses. And the two unite.

But *are* they quite united? Don't they want
to take this path together? Even now,
from house to field both are kept from speaking.

Even celestial signs can be deceiving.
For just a little while, though, let's allow
ourselves to trust the image. This is enough.

I.12

P raise to the spirit who can find a way
    of binding us, because we live in figures.
Clocks march with measured paces, and the minutes
    tick off alongside our momentous day.

Of where we really are we're unaware,
    and yet we act as though it all pertains.
Antennas feel for other antennas, with
    a sense across the empty distances. . . .

Electric tension. Music of pure force!
    Doesn't our petty business interfere
with your remote transmission on the air?

For all his worried labor and concern,
    the farmer never digs to where seeds turn
deep soil into summer. Earth *bestows*.

I.13

Full ripe apple, banana and pear,
    gooseberry. . . . All of them speak
of death and life in the mouth, I feel. . . .
    Gather this from a child's face,

devouring. It comes from far away.
    What's growing slowly nameless in your mouth?
In place of words, new drifts are found,
    released from the fruit's pulp, amazed.

Just try to say what "apple" means.
    This concentrated sweetness is growing
transparent, lucid, wide-awake,

emerging with a salient taste.
    Two-sided, sunny, earthy, here—
experience, feeling, joy—enormous!

I.14

We are involved in flower, vine, and fruit:
    they speak not only the language of the year.
Out of the dark appears a leafy shoot,
    its green suggestive of the jealous leer

of those now dead who fructify the earth.
    About their part in this, what can we know?
For so long they have brought about the birth
    of clay, with the stray marrow of their bones.

So here's the question: is it gladly done? . . .
    Or is this fruit a clenched fist raised by slaves,
worn down by toil, toward us, the ones above?

Or could *they* be in charge, asleep in graves
    beside the roots, and giving from their surfeit
this hybrid of mute vigor and of kisses?

I.15

Wait . . . this flavor . . . it's already fading.
  A piece of music, stamping feet, a hum—
young women, with your silences inflamed,
  now dance for what you know is on your tongue!

Dance the orange. Who cannot remember
  the way it labors, drowning in its own
sweetness? So delectable and tender,
  after this conversion it is yours.

Dance the orange. Throw its warmer landscape
  away from you, until the ripeness shines
amid these native breezes! Peel away

each aroma, making new relations
  with the pure, the self-restraining rind,
and with the flavorable juice inside!

1.16

You, man's best friend, are so alone,
        because . . . with words and fingertips
we gradually make the world our own,
        including its most delicate bits.

Who points a finger toward a scent?
        Out of the powers that cause us alarm,
you feel many . . . you know the dead
        and cower before the sorcerer's charm.

See, both of us must always bear
        patches and scraps, as if complete.
To help you is hard. Don't plant me in

your heart, for I would grow too deep.
        But I'll guide *my* master's hand and say:
here, this is Esau in his skin.

I.17

Under all well-founded things,
    entangled root that lies
hidden, as the secret spring
    from which they arise.

War helmet, horn of the gunners,
    age-weary truths,
wrath among brothers,
    and women like lutes . . .

The branches cramp each other,
    none of them free —
but one! Climb — go higher . . .

Still, they break one another.
    At the top of the tree,
one bends into a lyre.

1.18

D o you hear the New, mister,
  rumble and quake?
Here come the announcers
    to herald its name.

There *is* no safe hearing
    amidst the uproar,
but all this machinery
    needs our support.

See the Machine:
    it turns and gets revenge,
leaving us impaired.

Yet *we* give it strength,
    so let it be restrained
to propel and serve.

1.19

Despite the ferment of the world,
    changing like the shapes of clouds,
all completed things return
    home to their primordial ground.

Above change and wandering,
    more free and higher,
your overture still endures,
    god of the lyre.

Suffering hasn't been fathomed,
    nor love understood,
and that which death erases

remains no less obscure.
    Song alone over the land
keeps holy and praises.

I.20

Y ou, who make all creatures able to hear,
        oh poet, tell me: what can I dedicate
to you? I remember one spring day,
        near dusk, in Russia, when a horse appeared—

Across the village he came up alone,
        all white, a hobble fettering one leg,
to camp out in the pasture on his own;
        how that curled mane beat against his neck,

keeping time with his animated spirit—
        despite the awkwardly impeded gallop.
And how his stallion-blood rushed from the source!

He felt the open distances. He sang
        and listened—and your cycle of songs became
complete in him. This image: it is yours.

I.21

S pring is arriving back again. The earth
is like a child reciting many poems
she's memorized by heart. Her prize is worth
the effort spent on what is now disclosed.

Her teacher was severe. We loved the white
hair all throughout the old man's hoary beard.
Now we can ask her what green colors might
mean, or blue: and she knows every word!

Fortunate earth, enjoy your holiday—
play with the kids, and watch us try in vain
to catch you. Only the happiest survives.

O, her teacher has shown so many things:
all that's written in roots, and all the signs
inscribed on intricate twigs. And now she sings!

I.22

What's driving is us;
    yet the pace of time
is nothing but dust
    next to what abides.

For everything hurried,
    it's already night.
Only the enduring
    can sanction our life.

O children, don't waste
    your bravery in racing
around or being flighty.

All things now stay put:
    darkness and brightness,
both flower and book.

I.23

O nly *then*, when flight
  no more for its own sake
ascends into the still sky,
    sufficient, self-contained,

so that it gleams again,
    with contours well-designed,
to play the lover of the wind,
    secure, lean, and alive—

not until a pure frontier
    outweighs puerile complacency
about the latest contrivance

will someone, flushed with victory
    and bringing distant places near,
be what he is alone in flying.

I.24

S hall we disown our oldest friendships, those
    vast undemanding deities, since that
hard metal we have tempered never chose
        to know them? Or try to find them on a map?

All of these potent friends, who take the dead
        from us—they never even touch our wheels.
We've moved too far away: our baths and feasts
        take place beyond their messengers. Ahead,

we leave them in the dust. Now, more alone,
        not knowing one another, we depend
on what we do not know. Our roads are straight,

and don't meander back upon themselves.
        The pistons lift in boilers where the old
flame burns. Yet, as we swim, our powers fail.

I.25

B ut *you*, whom I knew like a flower whose name
I didn't know, you were somehow bound to die,
and *now* I will recall you, show you to them,
    gorgeous playfellow of the unthwarted cry.

Dancer at first, whose body hesitated,
    then stopped — as if her youth were cast in bronze.
Lamentation, listening. Then, from the great
    makers, music fell into her altered heart.

Sickness was near. Already mastered by shadows,
    her darkened blood, suspicious, couldn't wait;
it surged forth toward its natural springtime.

Again and again, through darkness and disaster,
    it glowed, earthly. Only horrible beating
sent it through the hopelessly open gate.

1.26

And you, divine one, sounding until the end,
even when besieged by a swarm of maenads—
you beautifully drowned out their violent yell,
a voice of order prevailing over the chaos.

None of them could destroy your head or harp,
however much they struggled. All of the sharp
stones thrown in rage at you turned soft upon
approaching, suddenly able to hear your song.

At last they killed you, in retaliation,
but in the aftermath your music rings—
in rocks and trees, in lions and birds you sing.

O, vanished god! Your everlasting mark!
since their hatred has torn you apart,
we alone are the ears and mouth of nature.

2.01

Breathing, you unseeable poem!
Constantly in exchange between
our existence and the space of the world.
    Counterweight where I rhythmically come to be.

Solitary wave, in which
    I am the gradual sea.
Most sparing of all possible seas, you win
    space eventually.

How many places have already been
    inhaled by me—many a wind
is like my own child.

Do you know me, air, full of my traces?
    You were once the trunk, rind,
and greenery of my phrases.

2.02

S ometimes a scrap of paper close at hand
    is canvas for the master's *genuine* work;
so mirrors often capture in a glance
        the sacred and distinctive smiles of girls

as they survey the morning, all alone—
        or, in the hidden glow of indoor lights.
What real and breathing faces later show
        is just a dim reflection or disguise.

These eyes that look into the blackening coals
        of a slow-dying fire: what have they seen?
Glimpses of life, forever exhausted.

Earth, who comprehends your losses?
        Only the one who nonetheless can sing
in praise, with heart delivered into the whole.

2.03

Mirrors: no one has ever yet described
your essence, for we don't know what it is.
You fill the intervening space of time
    as openly as holes throughout a sieve.

You are the wastrels in the vacant hall—
    when twilight arrives, wide as a grove of trees.
And, like a trophy stag, the luster vaults
    across your inaccessible boundary.

Often you are filled with pictures. Some
    appear to have already entered you,
while others you have gently sent away.

But she remains, the most beautiful one,
    until Narcissus finally breaks through
and makes his way to her concealed face.

2.04

This is the animal that does not exist.
    They didn't know it, and—in any case,
they loved it—neck and footsteps, even its
    demeanor and the light of its mild gaze.

It never did exist. But from their love
    this pure being came to be. They gave it room,
and in that clear space, desolate enough,
    it raised its head up out of the cocoon

of nonexistence. So they fed it, not
    with grain, but with the possibility
of being. And the creature grew so strong,

out of its brow a single horn emerged.
    All white, it showed up for a girl, and she
perceived it—in the mirror, and in her.

2.05

Flower-flesh, unfolding bit by bit
    this anemone in the meadow dawn,
until its loins are open to the light
    of many sounds the loud sky gushes down;

muscle of infinite receptivity,
    you flex within the silent flower-star,
at times *so* overwhelmed by superfluity
    that the gentle beckoning and calm

of sunset can just barely realign
    all these hyperextended petal edges:
determination of *how many* worlds!

We violent ones, we finally endure.
    But *when* — that is, in which of all our lives,
can we at last be open and receptive?

2.06

Rose, enthroned one, you in ancient times
were just a flower with a simple cup.
Now you are the inexhaustible blossom,
    blooming on innumerably for us.

In your finery, you seem to be
    layers of clothes around a body made
of light; yet every petal is at once
    an undraped body nakedly displayed.

For centuries your scent has beckoned us,
    as if it whispered sweet familiar things;
then, suddenly, it fills the air like fame.

We guess your name, and yet we cannot know.
    Our memory is invaded by a fragrance,
summoning what we held in mind before.

2.07

F lowers, related at last to arranging hands
 (feminine hands, in the past and even still),
you often lay across the garden table,
  slightly injured and beginning to wilt,

waiting for the water that might revive you
  just a while, since death is setting in —
and now you're lifted up between the beams
  of sympathetic fingers once again,

whose gentle touch is able to support
  your waking in the vase. Then, as you cool
slowly, breathing out the warmth of girls,

draining like the taint of sins confessed,
  committed with your picking, you renew
a bond of kinship with your friends in bloom.

2.08

You few, my childhood playmates from a time
    now lost, dispersed in all the city gardens:
we found and, cautiously, began to like
    each other. As the lamb gives voice to darkness,

we spoke in silence. Then, when there was joy,
    nobody owned it: whose joy could it be?
We saw it dissolve beneath the people's noise
    and in the lengthy year's anxiety.

Unfamiliar vehicles wheeled past,
    and houses stood around us, strong but false—
none knew us. What was real under the sun?

Nothing. Only the balls. Their marvellous paths.
    Not even the children. . . . But sometimes one
would step, ephemeral, under the plummeting ball.

2.09

Y ou who judge, don't boast about omitting
   torture—even if irons are inconvenient.
No one's heart is comforted, because
      reluctant pangs of mercy made you lenient.

The scaffold will return what it's been given
      for ages, just as children often trade
their birthday gifts. The real god of mercy
      would find another manner to invade

the pure and open heart. He'd come to grip
      it firmly, bathed in godlike radiant light.
More than a wind for large, complacent ships.

Nothing less than a silent understanding
      that wins us over inwardly, at play
much like the child of some vast partnership.

2.10

All that we have gained, the machine threatens—
once a tool assumes a force of its own.
Instead of letting us get used to mastery,
    for buildings more severe it cuts the stone.

Nowhere does it pause and allow us to flee,
    maintaining itself and leaving factories hushed.
It thinks itself alive—and with the same
    state of mind it makes, arrays, destructs.

But life for us is still enchanted, in
    a hundred places new. Pure force at play,
which strikes whoever sees it with amazement.

Words continue to fail before the nameless. . . .
    And music, always new in vacant space,
builds a cobbled house where gods can live.

2.11

Many a peacefully-rendered rule of death
    came from the hunting of these desperados;
strip of cloth, I know you better than net
    or trap: they hung you down in the Carso grottos.

They lowered you gently, gesturing (as it were)
    in peace. But then their helper gave a tug,
and from the caves night flung a handful of birds,
    dazed by the glare . . .
                  And *this* is somehow just.

Let any breath of regret be far from these
    who oversee, not only the vigilant hunter,
who handily executes when the time arrives.

Killing is one form of our homeless grief . . .
    Whatever may happen to us
turns pure in the radiant mind.

2.12

S eek transformation, yearning for the flame
  in which proud alterations must be burned;
the spirit who charts out Earth's blueprint craves
    above all points the one where something turns.

What sticks to mere survival soon gets rigid:
    how safe is it to hide in a gray backyard?
Look—far away, an absent hammer is lifted.
    The hardest sends forewarning to the hard.

Whoever overflows is known by Knowing;
    she leads him, transfixed, through the fair creation
that often ends at the start and begins at the end.

Each happy space they walk through in amazement
    is Exit's child or grandchild. And the transformed,
laurel Daphne wants you to turn into wind.

2.13

Be ahead of all parting, just as if
it lay behind you like a passing season.
Among the winters, one (*so* endless) winter
   will leave your over-wintering heart unbeaten.

Be forever dead in your love—but sing,
   rise back up, and affirm the pure engagement.
Amid these fading and decaying things,
   be the glass that rings out as it's breaking.

Be—but know the terms and limitations
   of not-being, ground of your intimate vibration,
so that you fully meet them, even once.

Jubilantly with all that is dumb or deadened,
   the unsayable whole of nature's plenty,
number yourself as well—and annul the sum.

2.14

Perceive these flowers, faithful to the earth,
  to which we lend a destiny from the edge
of fate—but who knows? If they face decay,
  it's up to us to feel their regret.

All things arise. We trudge, as if weighed down,
    pressing on everything, entranced with gravity.
What dreary teachers! Badly out of tune
    with all that dwells in childhood everlasting.

And yet if someone brought them into sleep
    completely, slept with things—how he'd awake
into a different day, from that same deep.

Or maybe he would stay; and they would thrive,
    admitting him, a convert, to live among
his siblings in the field where calm air sweeps.

2.15

O fountain-mouth, you never-ending giver,
    with lips that always speak of one clear thing—
you marble mask faced up against the stream
    of water. And way off there in the distance,

the origin of aqueducts. Out where
    those gravestones lie, behind the Apennines,
they carry back to you your liquid sayings,
    which flow down past your old, black chin to find

themselves cascading into the basin there.
    This is the ear laid on its side in slumber,
the marble ear to which your voice is given.

An ear of Earth. Although she's by herself,
    she's always talking: dip in with a pitcher,
and it will seem as if you interrupt her.

2.16

Always torn apart by us again,
Orpheus is still the place of healing.
We're all sharp-edged, because we want to know,
but he (the god) is widespread and serene.

Even the pure, the sacred offering,
is taken into his world no other way
except as he himself stands opposite
the open ending, motionless and staid.

Those alone who are dead are drinking
from this spring that's *heard* by us,
when the god provides a secret hint.

To *us*, only the noise is given.
And the lamb asks for the bell it wants
by virtue of a more quiet instinct.

2.17

Where, in what blissfully-watered gardens,
    on which trees, from what soft opening blossoms
do the wild fruits of solace ripen? Precious
    fruit, which may be found in the trampled meadows

of your losses. Time and again, you find
    yourself astonished by the size of the fruit,
by its wholeness and its unbroken rind—
    and no lax bird or jealous worm at the root

has taken it. Are there trees where angels gather,
    cultivated by slow, unknowable gardeners,
that give us fruit although they are not ours?

We soon grow ripe, then wither, just like phantoms
    or shadows. Don't we ever possess the power
to ruffle the stillness of these tranquil summers?

2.18

Dancer: o you translation
of all things fleeting into steps.
And how! That last whirl, tree of motion—
    wasn't the sweep of the year possessed?

Didn't the wavering swarm at its top,
    all in blossom, at once become calm?
Overhead, wasn't it summer and sun,
    from your measureless radiant warmth?

It also bore your tree of ecstasy.
    Aren't these its peaceful fruits: the urn,
with its ripening bars, and the seasoned vase?

And in these pictures: doesn't the sketch endure,
    the dark line of your eyebrows pencilling
quick—across the turning page?

2.19

G old resides in some indulgent bank,
  intimate with many. But for the blind
beggar, a copper coin is like a place
      that's lost, a dusty corner he can't find.

Money feels right at home in all the stores;
      it struts by, dressed in silk, fur, and carnations.
He, the silent one, dwells within the lulls
      that breathing money makes, asleep or awakened.

How can it close, that ever-open hand?
      When the night ends, fate brings it out once more:
wretched, easily destructible.

Until some shocked onlooker understands,
      and praises its duration. A singer can say.
Only for a god is it audible.

2.20

How far between the stars; and yet, much farther
are the distances that we grasp this instant.
Just look at any child . . . and then, another
— o how inexpressibly distant.

Maybe fate measures us in spans of being,
and for this reason it seems inauspicious;
How many spans might separate the woman
who flees from that same man she also wishes.

All is far; the circle's incomplete.
Look at that fish waiting for us to eat:
how strange is its expression in the dish!

Fish are mute . . . or so we thought. Who knows?
Isn't there a place where the language of the fish,
or what it would be, can at last be spoken?

2.21

S ing, my heart, of gardens you've never known;
 clear, inaccessible, as if encased
in glass. Waters and roses of Shiraz
     or Isfahan: rejoice, for they are graced

supremely. Show that you cannot do without them,
     and that their figs are ripening for you.
You are familiar with the winds among
     the pregnant branches looming into view.

Avoid the mistake of thinking you offended
     fate through this decision: to exist!
Silk thread, into the fabric you were blended.

Whatever shape you inwardly go into
     (even one moment from a life of pain),
know that the whole tapestry is intended.

2.22

O despite fate: the lavish extravagance
     of our existence, gushing like fountains in parks
—or taking form as stone men propping up
     tall entrances, and under lofty walks!

And the bronze bell, lifting up its hammer
     against the dull routine of everydayness. . . .
Or at Karnak that column there—the one
     that has outlasted temples that are ancient.

Today those same abundances will race
     away, the fast ones, going straight across
from yellow day to overwhelming night.

The frenzy passes by without a trace.
     But they survive, those lovely arcs of flight
and those who made them—only in our thoughts.

2.23

Summon me to that one among your hours
which resists you, time and time again:
as a dog's face gently begs, then cowers,
    turning away (it always does) just when

you think at last that it's within your reach.
    What's taken away like this is most your own;
we're free, because we found ourselves released
    just where we thought of being welcomed home.

Anxiously we grapple for a hold—
    sometimes, we're too young for what is old
and too old for that which never was.

Still, it's only fair to praise, because:
    oh, nonetheless. We are the metal, and
the sweet that looms and ripens on the branch.

2.24

O this ever-new urge, from loosened soil!
   At first, no one would help those daring few;
but still, on lucky gulfs, the cities grew
      and jugs filled nonetheless with water and oil.

Gods: we draw them first in the boldest colors,
      which sullen fate eventually destroys.
And yet they *are* immortal. Our reward
      is to hear that one who attends to us.

We are one generation through the ages,
      fathers and mothers filled with kids to come
so that, at last, we shall be overtaken.

We, always daring—Time is never done!
      And only silent Death can keep in mind
the victory he wins by lending time.

2.25

L isten—already you can hear at work
    the first plows turning, and the gentle strum
of human measures on the pregnant earth
    before a robust spring. What's bound to come

does not seem free of taste. What often showed
    itself before appears to come anew,
as something else. Forever well-disposed,
    you never took it in: but it took you.

Even the leaves of wintering trees reveal
    a glimpse at dusk presaging later brown.
Sometimes, even the winds make their appeal.

Black are the bushes. Still, the heaps of dung
    stand blacker all across the fertile ground.
And each elapsing hour grows more young.

2.26

How we are moved by the call of a bird . . .
or any other cry, once it's been made.
Even the brightest kids, who play
    out in the open, surpass what's actually heard.

Contingent scream. In all these gaps between,
    this world-space (where bird-cries enter
unashamed, as men go into dreams) —
    their shrieks are driven in, like wedges.

Alas, where are we? Always more free,
    and laughter-edged, like kites with broken string,
we range halfway across the sky —

wind-ripped. O Poet, orchestrate all those
    who cry: may they awaken with a roar,
one current carrying both head and lyre.

2.27

Is there such a thing as Time the destroyer?
    When will it wreck the tower on the mountain?
As for this heart, so far divinely owned,
    when does it fall to the Demiurge's power?

Are we really so anxiously breakable
    as our Destiny seems to indicate?
Must childhood, so deep and capable,
    eventually get cut off at the base?

Ah, the ghost of transience—
    it goes right through the innocent
as if it were passing through haze.

And as for us, the ones who strive,
    the powers assign us a role to play
as part of the godly enterprise.

2.28

O come and go. You, still a child almost,
  perform a dance in the blink of an eye, creating
a pure constellation—one of those
    devices by which orderly, blunt Nature

is momently surpassed. For she was stirred
    to total hearing only by Orphic song.
You were inspired from the time you heard,
    and thought it odd if any tree stood long

before it joined you in the space of hearing.
    You still remember where the lyre arose,
intoning—from that middlemost location.

Therefore, you took exquisite steps, and hoped
    eventually to bring your friend to peer
and step into the sacred celebration.

2.29

Quiet friend of many distances,
    feel how your breath is creating room.
Among the rafters of dark belfries let
    yourself ring out. Whatever's eating you

is growing strong upon this offering.
    Give way to transformation every time.
What experience brings your deepest suffering?
    If your drinking is bitter, turn to wine.

In this comprehensive night, become
    the junction where all senses intermix;
be the truth of their odd rendezvous.

And if the world has forgotten you,
    say this to the stable earth: I run.
Tell the rushing water: I exist.